THE YORKSHIRE
COLOURING BOOK

First published 2016
Reprinted 2017, 2018, 2019, 2021, 2022, 2024

The History Press
97 St George's Place,
Cheltenham, GL50 3QB
www.thehistorypress.co.uk

British Library Cataloguing in Publication Data.
A catalogue record for this book is available from the British Library.

ISBN 978 0 7509 6811 9

Cover colouring by Lucy Hester.
Typesetting and origination by The History Press
Printed by Thomson Press, India

THE YORKSHIRE
COLOURING BOOK

PAST AND PRESENT

Take some time out of your busy life to relax and unwind with this feel-good colouring book designed for everyone who loves Yorkshire.

Absorb yourself in the simple action of colouring in the scenes and settings from around the county of Yorkshire, past and present. From iconic architecture to picturesque moorland vistas, you are sure to find some of your favourite locations waiting to be transformed with a splash of colour. Bring these scenes alive as you de-stress with this inspiring and calming colouring book.

There are no rules – choose any page and any choice of colouring pens or pencils you like to create your own unique, colourful and creative illustrations.

Little Shambles, York ▸

Kirklees Light Railway, Huddersfield ▸

Tolson Museum, Huddersfield ▶

Kiplin Hall, North Yorkshire ▸

Brontë Parsonage Museum, Haworth ▸

Ripon Workhouse Museum ▸

Bandstand, Weston Park ▶

The Yorkshire Dales ▶

Millennium Gallery, Sheffield ▸

North Bay Railway, Scarborough ▸

Selby Abbey ▶

Wakefield Cathedral, late 1960s ▸

Doncaster, *c.* 1900 ▶

Burnby Hall Gardens, Pocklington ▸

Barnsley Town Hall ▸

The Streetlife Museum of Transport,
Kingston-upon-Hull ▸

Bridlington Old Town ▸

Bingley Five Rise Locks ▶

Hull Maritime Museum ▶

North York Moors Railway ▸

Bishops' House, Sheffield ▶

Scarborough beach and Grand Hotel, 1890s ▸

The interior of Beverley Minster ▶

Knaresborough Castle ▶

Saltburn Pier ▶

Conduit Court, Skipton Castle ▶

Whitby harbour ▶

York Minster ▸

Yorkshire women walking dogs, *c.* 1900 ▸

Scarborough Castle ▶

The interior of Ripon Cathedral ▸

Saltaire Salts Mill ▶

Rievaulx Abbey, Helmsley ▸

Sheep being herded through Hawes, 1960s ▸

Castle Howard, North Yorkshire ▸

Brodsworth Hall and Gardens, Doncaster ▸

Roseberry Topping, North Yorkshire ▸

Fountains Abbey, Ripon ▶

Leeds Corn Exchange interior ▶

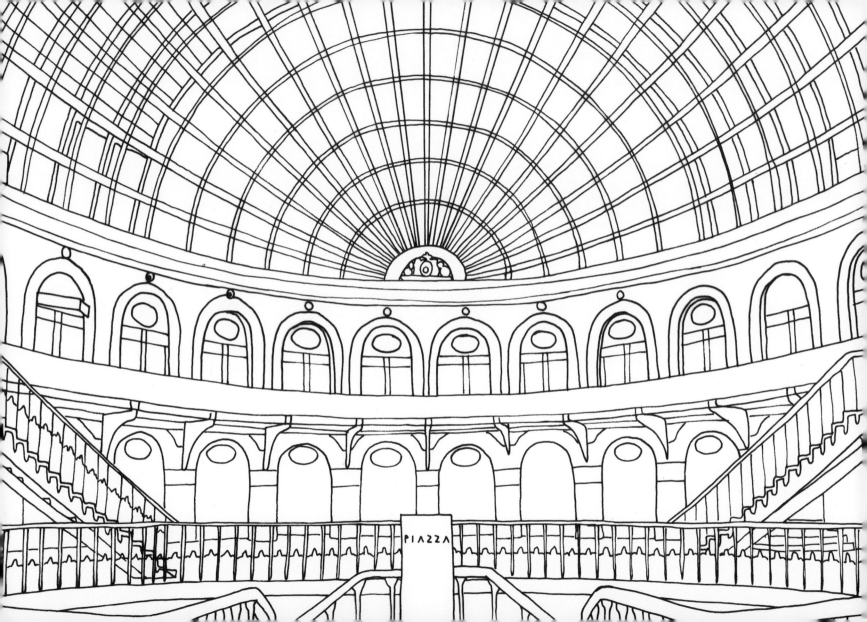

Cartwright Hall, Bradford ▶

Barley Hall, York ▶

Fisher girls, Scarborough, 1909 ▸

Royal Pump Room Museum, Harrogate ▸

The People's Park, Halifax, *c.* 1930 ▸

Whitby Abbey ▶

Also from The History Press

THE NORTHUMBERLAND
C O L O U R I N G   B O O K

PAST AND PRESENT